W9-AMA-650

Davidson
17.95
7/29/13

This library edition published in 2012 by Walter Foster Publishing, Inc.
Distributed by Black Rabbit Books.
P.O. Box 3263 Mankato, Minnesota 56002

Designed and published by Walter Foster Publishing, Inc.
Walter Foster is a registered trademark.

Printed in Mankato, Minnesota, USA by CG Book Printers, a division of Corporate Graphics.

First Library Edition

        Library of Congress Cataloging-in-Publication Data

Watch me draw Dora's favorite adventures : let's draw! / illustrated by
Dave Aikins. -- 1st Library Edition
        pages cm
  At head of title: Nick Jr. Dora the Explorer
  ISBN 978-1-936309-76-4
  1. Cartoon characters--Juvenile literature. 2.
Drawing--Technique--Juvenile literature. 3. Dora the Explorer
(Television program)--Juvenile literature. I. Aikins, Dave, illustrator.
II. Title: Dora's favorite adventures : let's draw! III. Title: Nick Jr.
Dora the Explorer.
  NC1764.W377 2012
  741.5'1--dc23
                        2012004014

052012
17679

9 8 7 6 5 4 3 2 1

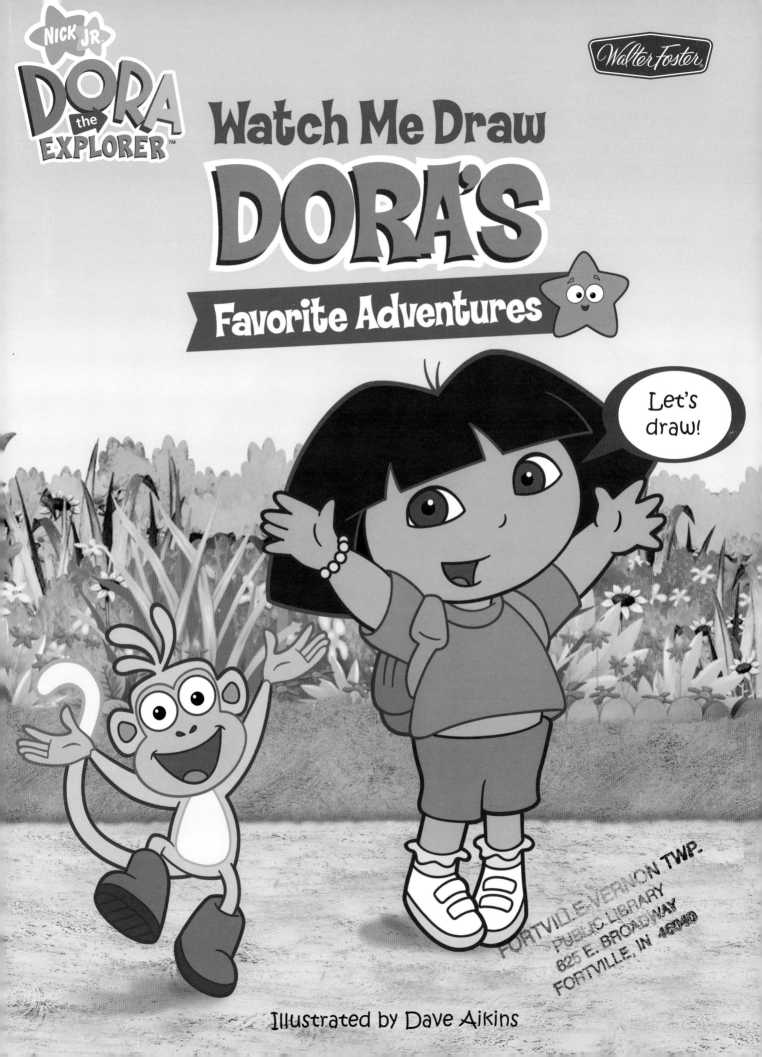

Illustrated by Dave Aikins

¡Hola! My name is Dora. I like to go on adventures with my best friend, Boots. We've gone on some really great adventures together— like the time we brought a little red fish back to his home.

Draw the fish! ¡El pez!

1

2

3

4

5

6

One time, I went on an adventure to my Abuela's house to help her make delicious cookies!

Draw the cookie! ¡La galleta!

On a lot of my adventures, I pass Isa's Flowery Garden. Look at all the beautiful flowers! How many flowers do you see?

Draw the flower! ¡La flor!

Every time I go exploring, that sneaky fox Swiper tries to swipe my stuff. Do you see Swiper?

Draw the tree! ¡El árbol!

Sometimes it's an adventure just staying home and being
a big sister. I love my baby brother and sister so much.
I even let them play with my favorite teddy bear.

Draw the teddy bear! ¡El osito!

Remember when you helped me on an adventure
to return Little Star to the night sky so all our friends
could make wishes? Let's make a wish together!

Draw the star! ¡La estrella!

Even a day at the beach can turn into a great adventure. Boots and I like to build sand castles.

Draw the sand castle! ¡El castillo de arena!

Some of our adventures have been out of this world! Remember the time you helped us blast off on a rocket ship to return our space creature friends to The Purple Planet?

Draw the rocket ship! ¡El cohete espacial!

Backpack carries everything I need on all my adventures, even on my adventures to school. Will you help me find all my books so Backpack can carry them to school?

Draw the book! ¡El libro!

I love it when we explore music with my friends,
like the time we all joined a musical parade!
I like to play the guitar!

Draw the guitar! ¡La guitarra!

Sometimes I get to explore new lands, like Fairytale Land!
In Fairytale Land, I met a giant, a king and queen,
and even a dragon!

Draw the dragon! ¡El dragón!

Exploring is exciting, but do you know what my favorite part is? Celebrating the end of each adventure with my friends! ¡Mis amigos!